Love,
Earth

by Jeffrey Turner

Edited and Designed by Brian Scott Sockin

ISBN: 978-1-943978-60-1

Printed in CHINA
cpsia tracking label information
Production Location: Rightol, China
Production Date: 10/24/2022
Cohort: Batch No. F2C0163547

10 9 8 7 6 5 4 3 2 1

PERSNICKETY
PRESS

Produced by Persnickety Press
An imprint of WunderMill, inc.
321 Glen Echo Lane, Suite C
Cary, NC 27518
www.persnickety-press.com

WunderMill

Love,
Earth

PERSNICKETY PRESS

This book is dedicated to the children of the world who will lead the charge in protecting and loving our sweet earth.

— Jeffrey Turner

Dear Reader...

My name is Earth.
I am very old.

Just like someone who is really old,

sometimes I need a little help. That's where you come in.

Plant a tree. Or two.

Trees provide

oxygen and improve air quality. We need more of them.

Use less energy.

Turn down the heat. Put on a sweater to

keep warm when it gets chilly inside the house.

Plant a flower garden.

Flowers attract bees.

Bees collect

pollen and help flowers make seeds.

Bring the outdoors inside.

Indoor plants

TEA

clean the air pollution inside your house.

Give your old sweaters and t-shirts to an animal shelter.

They can be used

Grow clover or meadows, not lawns.

Lawn mowers

dirty the air.

Give away the clothes
you've outgrown.

You'll reduce

waste by not throwing them

If you find
an ant in your house,
take it outside and
let it go.

Ants spread seeds

and seeds sprout into

Put trash in trash cans, not on the ground.

Littering hurts

the environments where animals live.

Set up a
rain barrel to
collect water.

Use the rainwater to

Turn off
the lights
you aren't
using.

It saves energy and

lets me share the starry night skies with my migratory friends.

And most
important,
please share.

Sharing lets you

take care of each other and me. Love, Earth

Taking care of the Earth can be fun.

Grow some air.
Put soil in a paper egg container and start growing plants from seeds.
The container will break down to make the soil better and the plants give us fresh air.

Get crafty.
Decorate a can with buttons from old shirts.

Make a bird happy.
Create a bird feeder from a toilet paper roll covered in peanut butter and seeds.

Can you think

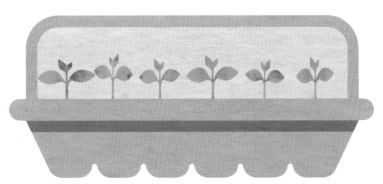

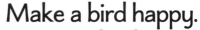

Decorate a metal water bottle with stickers to make it yours (instead of using and throwing away plastic water bottles). That will save plastic from going to the dump.

of more fun ways to help keep Earth healthy?

Start a worm farm. Worms eat kitchen scraps and turn them into fertilizer for plants.